Report on the Barnhouse Effect

Kurt Vonnegut Jr.

GOGAKU SHUNJUSHA

This book is published in Japan
by Gogaku Shunjusha Co., Inc.
2-9-10 Misaki-cho, Chiyoda-ku
Tokyo

First published 2006
© Gogaku Shunjusha Co., Inc.
Printed in Japan, All rights reserved.

はしがき

　言語の学習にはテレビ，ビデオよりもラジオやＣＤのほうがはるかに適しているといわれる。それは音だけが唯一のコミュニケーションの手段だからだ。映像がない分，耳の働きは一層鋭敏になり，聴きとる力は確実にアップする。それは理論的にも証明済みである。

　アメリカで制作されたこの『イングリッシュ・トレジャリー（英語の宝箱）』は，その観点からリスニングの究極の教材といえるだろう。

　英米の名作，傑作が放送ドラマ形式で作られているので，登場人物のセリフがまるで目の前でしゃべっているかのように聞こえてくる。しかも，効果音が実によく挿入されているので，胸に迫る臨場感は格別だ。一瞬たりともリスナーの耳を離さないすばらしい出来栄えである。

　しかも，ドラマの出演者は，アメリカ・ハリウッド黄金時代を飾ったスターたちだ。人の言葉とはこんなに魅力あるものかと，あらためて感動を呼ぶ。

　『イングリッシュ・トレジャリー』のよさは，またその構成のうまさにあるといえよう。物語の進行に伴う場面ごとに適切なナレーションが入って，ストーリーの背景を説明してくれるので，リスナーの耳は瞬時にその場面に引き込まれる。そして，会話によどみがない。

　名作を十分堪能しながら，同時に総合的な語学学習ができるところに，この教材の利点がある。

　「リスニング力」の上達はもちろん，ストーリーの中で覚えられる「単語・会話表現」，そしてシャドウ（あとからついて言う）もでき，かつ，英語シナリオ一本まるごと読むことで身につく「読解力」と，まさに一石三鳥，いや四鳥の「英語の宝箱」だ。

　どの作品を取り上げても文句なく楽しめるシリーズだ。

CONTENTS

はしがき……………………………………… iii
シリーズの使用法…………………………… v
CD INDEX 一覧……………………………… vi
解　説………………………………………… vii
ものがたり…………………………………… ix
SCENE 1 ……………………………………… 2
SCENE 2 ……………………………………… 24
SCENE 3 ……………………………………… 32
SCENE 4 ……………………………………… 42
SCENE 5 ……………………………………… 44
SCENE 6 ……………………………………… 52
SCENE 7 ……………………………………… 54
SCENE 8 ……………………………………… 58
SCENE 9 ……………………………………… 62
SCENE10 ……………………………………… 64
SCENE11 ……………………………………… 70
SCENE12 ……………………………………… 76

●シリーズの使用法

英検1級レベル

　まず，英文シナリオを見ずにCDに耳を集中する。第2ステージでは，聞き取れなかった部分及び「これは」と思った慣用表現を英文シナリオでチェック。最終的には口頭でシャドウできるまで習熟することが目標です。

英検2級〜準1級レベル

　英文シナリオを参照しながら，CDを聴くことから始める。第2ステージでは，英文シナリオの完全理解を図る。と同時に，重要な会話表現や単語をどんどん身につけていく。第3ステージでは，対訳を参照しながら，CDを聴いてみよう。シナリオなしにCDが聞き取れるようになれば卒業だ。

英検3級〜準2級レベル

　対訳を参照しながら，まず英文シナリオをしっかり読む。第2ステージでは，英文シナリオを参照しながらCDを聴こう。音声のスピードに慣れるまでは，章ごとに切って，何度も聴きながら，学習を進めてください。未知の単語や会話表現をどんどん覚えるチャンスです。

　第3ステージでは，対訳を参照しながら，CDに集中する。この頃には，耳も相当慣れてきて，リスニングにかなりの手応えが感じられてくるだろう。

　物語の選択にあたっては，難易度表の「初級〜中級レベル」表示の比較的易しめのものから入っていくことをお勧めする。

CD INDEX 一覧

	本文ページ	該当箇所	冒頭部分
1	2	**SCENE 1**	The mind of man is still an unprobed field.
2	24	**SCENE 2**	Professor Barnhouse mailed his letter, and…
3	32	**SCENE 3**	YDR to Brainwave Control.
4	42	**SCENE 4**	Barnhouse was gone, and within twelve hours…
5	44	**SCENE 5**	Look, Major Guthro, I told the FBI and…
6	52	**SCENE 6**	You say you do recognize this photograph,…
7	54	**SCENE 7**	Oh, brother, it's hot. What a way to spend…
8	58	**SCENE 8**	Sorry, gents, we're full.
9	62	**SCENE 9**	Here we are. Ward fifteen. This way…
10	64	**SCENE 10**	Every time I walk into this study,…
11	70	**SCENE 11**	Where are we headed? He didn't say…
12	76	**SCENE 12**	So, they brought me back here to…

（本CDは歴史的に貴重なオリジナル音源を使用しておりますので、一部お聴きぐるしい箇所が含まれている場合もございますが、ご了承ください）

解　説

　カート・ヴォネガット・ジュニア（Kurt Vonnegut Jr.）は1922年11月11日，ドイツ系移民の四世としてインディアナ州インディアナポリスに生まれた。

　コーネル大学在学中には，生化学を学ぶ一方，学内紙の編集局長などを務める。

　1944年，母エディスが自殺。同年，アメリカ合衆国第106歩兵隊員として第二次世界大戦のドイツ戦線に参加するが，捕虜となり，連行されたドレスデンで，同盟軍による「ドレスデン大空襲」を体験する。

　戦地から帰還した1945年よりシカゴ大学大学院で人類学を学び，MA（学位）を得ている。

　1947年からジェネラル・エレクトリック社で働いていたが，1950年，本書の原作となった短編「バーンハウス効果に関する報告書」（*Report on the Barnhouse Effect*）でSF作家としてデビュー。翌1951年マサチューセッツ州に居を移して，専業作家となる。

　日本では，1960年代後半から彼の作品が精力的に翻訳・紹介され，80年代には「ヴォネガット・ブーム」が巻き起こった。1984年には来日もしている。

　初期の頃には"SF作家"というレッテルを貼られて彼の発想やブラック・ユーモアは好意的に解釈されず，一般に悪評しか得られなかった。やがて，『スローターハウス５』に盛り込まれた，鋭い反戦の意志や人間無視の現代社会への抗議が，特に青年層の広い共感を呼び，それ以後，小説もエッセイも大歓迎を受けるようになった。いまや，現代アメリカ文学を代表する作家の１人といっても過言ではないだろう。

このドラマの原作は，前述のとおり，活字になった彼の作品の最初のものであるが，1950年2月，当時の人気週刊誌「コリヤーズ」に発表され，邦訳は下記の短篇集『モンキーハウスへようこそ』（早川書房）の中に収められている。
　主な作品には，以下のようなものがある。
『プレイヤー・ピアノ』（Player Piano：1950）
『タイタンの妖女』（The Sirens of Titan：1962）
『猫のゆりかご』（Cat's Cradle：1962）
『ローズウォーターさん，あなたに神のお恵みを』
　　　　　　　　　（God Bless You Mr. Rosewater：1965）
『モンキーハウスへようこそ』
　　　　　　　　　（Welcome to the Monkey House：1968）
『スローターハウス5』（Slaughterhouse-Five：1970）
『チャンピオンたちの朝食』（Breakfast of Champions：1973）
『スラップスティック』（Slapsticks：1976）
『ジェイルバード』（Jailbird：1979）
『デッドアイ・ディック』（Deadeye Dick：1982）

ものがたり

　1958年のことだった（原作では，近い未来という設定である）。ある小大学の助手として勤めることになったクリントンは，上司のバーンハウス教授が，何の仕事もせず居眠りばかりしているのに驚く。

　「自分の専門の心理研究を合衆国の役に立てるためにも，別の仕事につきたい」と申し出たクリントンに，教授は，「それなら自分の心を調べてみてほしい，正気を失いかけているようだから」と答える。教授には強力な"念動力"があって，サイコロの目を思い通りに操ることができるし，インク瓶だって遠く離れた所から破壊することができるように思う……しかし，それが自分でも本当とは思えないというのである。

　その言葉が事実だと確認したクリントンは，さっそく教授を説得し，国家のためにその力を振るわせようとする。ところが，これを絶好の強力破壊兵器としか解釈しない役人たちは，教授らを軍の関与する秘密計画に組み込んでしまい，この力を平和のために利用することなどおよそ考えてもみないのだった。あきれはてた教授は行方をくらまし，世界平和のため，たった1人で，無駄な軍拡を積み重ねる列強諸国の眼を覚まさせようとする。

　各国自慢の新秘密兵器が，次々と破壊され始めた。教授の仕業と気づいた国々は，何としても彼の行先をつきとめ，自らの陣営の利益のためにその力を利用しようとする。遂に捕えられた教授は，自ら命を絶つという道を選んだが……。

1

Narrator: The mind of man is still an unprobed field. Within it lie many mysteries still unsolved. But there are men today — psychologists now experimenting with telepathy, hypnosis, thought transference — who believe that in the future we may discover the existence of a force of the mind more powerful than any force the world has ever known.

We go ahead now in time some ten years; and in space, to the campus of a small eastern college. The hour is late. And in one of the dark college buildings, two men stand in front of the door that bears the name "Professor Arthur Barnhouse, Psychology."

Guthro: (*door is unlocked and opened*) Well, here you are, Clinton.

Clinton: Thank you, Major.

Guth: Here are the keys of the professor's desk and files. I guess you inherit

(1)

ナレーター： 　人間の心はまだまだ探求の及ばない領域で，そこには今なお解けない謎が数多く潜んでいる。しかし心理学者の中には，テレパシーや催眠術，思念伝達などの実験に取り組む人たちも多い。彼らは将来，人間の心に秘められた力——それも従来知られているどんな力よりも強大な力——の存在を突き止めることができる，と信じているのだ。

　ここで 10 年ほど未来へジャンプしてみよう。場所はアメリカ東部のこぢんまりとした大学のキャンパス。日は暮れている。暗い学舎の一棟の中で，とある部屋の前に 2 人の男が立っている。扉には「心理学教授　アーサー・バーンハウス」の名前が掲げられている。

ガスロ： 　（鍵を回してドアを開ける音）さあ，入りたまえ，クリントン君。
クリントン： 　恐縮です，少佐。
ガスロ： 　教授のデスクと書類戸棚の鍵だ。これで君がすべてを引き継いだことになる。まだ記憶が新しいうちに，詳しい報告書

everything now. You might as well dictate a full report while everything's still fresh in your mind. I'll wait and see you home.

Clint: Uh, no, no. That isn't necessary. I'll be all right.

Guth: You sure? After what's happened tonight, we wouldn't want you to have an accident, too.

Clint: Major, after what happened tonight, I have a hunch the whole world is ripe for an accident.

Guth: I'm afraid you're right, Clinton. Well, good night.

Clint: Good night. (*receding footsteps and closing door*) Ohhh, pull yourself together, Buster. Easy does it... August 21, 1960. Restrictive report from George Clinton to the Secretary of Defense, Secretary of State, the FBI, National Security Board, et cetera, et cetera, et cetera. Subject: the

	を口述しておいてはどうかね。終わるまで待って，家へ送ってあげよう。
クリントン:	いえ，それには及びません。1人で大丈夫です。
ガスロ:	そうかな？ 今晩あんな出来事があった直後だから，君も何かに巻き込まれないかと心配なんだが。
クリントン:	少佐，今晩あの出来事があった以上は，もうどこでどんな事件が起きてもおかしくありませんよ。
ガスロ:	そうかもしれんな，クリントン君。じゃ，失敬するよ。
クリントン:	お休みなさい。（遠ざかる足音，ドアを閉める音）さて，しっかりしなきゃな，落ち着くんだ。1960年8月21日。機密報告。報告者：ジョージ・クリントン，宛先：国防長官，国務長官，FBI，国家安全保障局，その他。件名：いわゆる「バーンハウス効果」とその発見者アーサー・バーンハウス教授について。

so-called Barnhouse Effect and Professor Arthur Barnhouse who discovered it.

I first met the professor two years ago in the fall of 1958. He was a professor of psychology here at Wilton College, and I was here on an instructor's fellowship in the psych department. They assigned me to be Barnhouse's assistant, and he needed one. He hardly ever remembered to go to a class and he didn't seem to do anything else, either. For three months, I watched him sitting at the desk here in his study. He'd either stare at nothing for hours or fall asleep, nodding over his mess of papers. I couldn't understand it, and it was none of my business; but one day, I thought I'd better give him a shake.

Barnhouse: Uhh, what? What?

Clint: I said, it's two-fifteen, Professor. Don't you want to go to your two-o'clock class?

Barn: Don't you want to mind your own business?

私が教授に初めて会ったのは2年前，1958年秋のことだった。教授はここウィルトン大学で心理学を教えており，私は心理学部の講師を務めていた。私はバーンハウス教授の助手に配属されたが，教授は助手なしではやっていけない状態だった。講義の予定は忘れてばかりで，まったく何も手につかない様子だったのだ。私は3カ月の間，教授がただこの研究室のデスクに座っているのを眺めていた。何時間も虚空を見つめているか，散らかった書類の上にがっくりと首を落として居眠りをする，といった具合だった。私にはそうした行動が理解できなかったが，私がどうこう言う筋合いでもない。しかしある日のこと，私は教授を揺り起こすことにした。

バーンハウス：　ん？　何だ，何だね？
クリントン：　もう2時15分ですよ，教授。2時からの講義に行かなくていいんですか？
バーンハウス：　君のほうこそ余計なお世話だとは思わんかね？

Clint: I beg your pardon.

Barn: Sorry, Clinton, forgive me. I don't know what gets into me. Forget the class. The kids would rather be outdoors anyway.

Clint: Okay, Professor. In that case, I'm sorry I woke you up.

Barn: Aw, it's all right. I just can't seem to get my sleeping done at night. Clinton, what do you know about the international situation?

Clint: Well, I'm no political scientist, if that's what you mean. I read the papers when I have time.

Barn: Well, that's the way I've always been. Lately, I've had to look into it. I stay up nights looking into it.

Clint: Uh, Professor, I don't want you to take this personally or anything, but... Well, sir, I wonder if you'd mind if I asked to be transferred?

クリントン:	そういう言い方はないんじゃないでしょうか。
バーンハウス:	悪かった，謝るよ，クリントン君。わしはどうかしとるな，まったく。講義のことは気にせんでもいい。どうせ子供は外で遊ぶほうがいいに決まっとる。
クリントン:	わかりました，教授。じゃあ，起こしてしまってすみませんでした。
バーンハウス:	なに，構わんさ。どうも夜はよく眠れないんでな。ところでクリントン君，国際情勢には通じておるかね？
クリントン:	政治学者ほど詳しくはありませんが，時間があれば新聞は読みます。
バーンハウス:	うん，わしもそうだった。しかし最近は詳しく知る必要に迫られてな，夜ふけまで調べ物をしてる。
クリントン:	あの，教授，どうか気を悪くされないように願いたいんですが，実は僕，配置換えをお願いしようと思ってるんです。

Barn: You mean you'd rather work with somebody else in the department?

Clint: Oh, no, sir, no, sir, it's not that. I, I think maybe there's a chance for a psychologist to work on that government project.

Barn: Government project? Ohh, yes, that army thing.

Clint: Yes, sir. They're trying to develop robot pilots for their new fighter rockets, so they'd be expendable.

Barn: Oh, yes, yes. Something else designed to replace men.

Clint: Yes, sir, and you know, it's a funny thing. The robots work just like human brains. They get overworked or overloaded or something, and they have nervous breakdowns. Now if I could only find out what drives those electronic brains crazy, why, I'd feel that I was...

Barn: Clinton, if you want to study a brain

バーンハウス： というと，学部内の別の教授につきたいのかね？

クリントン： いえ，そうではないんです。実は，例の政府プロジェクトで心理学者を募集しているらしいんです。

バーンハウス： 政府プロジェクト？ ああ，陸軍のやつかね？

クリントン： そうです。新型ロケット戦闘機を操るロボット・パイロットの開発を軍が進めているんです。ロボットならやられても補充できますからね。

バーンハウス： そうそう，人間の代わりがまた1つ増えるわけか。

クリントン： そうです，ところが面白いことに，このロボットは人間の脳とまったく同じように機能するので，疲れたりストレスがたまってノイローゼになってしまうんです。電子脳を狂わせる原因が何かを探り当てることができれば，きっと僕が……。

バーンハウス： クリントン君，狂いかけた脳ミソを研究したいんなら，ロ

that's going crazy, never mind the robots. You can go to work on me.

Clint: What are you talking about, sir?

Barn: I don't know. I'm either crazy as a bedbug, or a... Clinton, I wish you'd help me find out.

Clint: Are you serious, Professor?

Barn: I never was more serious in my life. I'm afraid I'm going out of my mind.

Clint: But, why? What makes you think so?

Barn: (*sound of dice rolled on desk top*) This is what makes me think I'm crazy.

Clint: Those dice?

Barn: Clinton, do you know what the odds are against my rolling a seven?

Clint: Oh, about five or six to one.

Barn: Watch. (*rolls dice*) Seven. Now, what are the odds against my rolling it again?

Clint: Twice in a row? Plenty. About a hundred to one, I'd say.

Barn: Watch. (*rolls dice*)

ボットなんか忘れなさい。わしを研究すればいい。

クリントン： どういうことですか？

バーンハウス： わしにもわからん。わしは気が狂っているのか，さもなければ……クリントン君，調べるのを手伝ってはくれんかね。

クリントン： 本気ですか，教授？

バーンハウス： ああ本気だとも。わしは気が変になってきたんじゃないかと心配してるんだ。

クリントン： でも，どうしてですか？ 何か思い当たる節でも？

バーンハウス： （机の上で2つのサイコロがころがる音）これじゃよ，わしがおかしくなったのかと心配する理由は。

クリントン： サイコロですか？

バーンハウス： クリントン君，サイコロ勝負で7への賭け率はいくらになるか知ってるかね？

クリントン： さあ，5，6倍でしょうか。

バーンハウス： 見てごらん。（サイコロを振る）7だ。さて，続けて7で勝負する場合の賭け率は？

クリントン： 2回続けてですか？ かなり高いですよ，100倍ぐらいじゃないですか。

バーンハウス： よくごらん。（サイコロを振る）

Clint: (*whistles*) **Professor, you're hotter than a two-dollar pistol.**

Barn: Heh, it's funny. That's what they said eight years ago when I first discovered this.

Clint: Discovered what?

Barn: This force of the mind. I call it dynamo psychism.

Clint: You mean you shove those dice around just by thinking about it?

Barn: People have always thought there could be a force of the mind. You know that. Fortunately, or unfortunately, I've learned to control it.

Clint: Yeah? Uh, how did you happen to find out about this, Professor?

Barn: Well, it was about ten years ago, back in 1948. I made a mistake of going to a psychologists' convention. And in order not to appear unsocial, I happened to find myself — for the first and only time in

クリントン: （口笛を吹く）教授，凄い腕前じゃないですか。

バーンハウス: ふん，面白いな。8年前にわしがこれを発見した時も，みんなそう言ったよ。

クリントン: 発見したって，何をですか。

バーンハウス: マインドパワーさ。わしはこれを念動力と呼んでいるがね。

クリントン: というと，考えるだけでサイコロを動かせるんですか？

バーンハウス: 心には力が潜んでいる，と昔から考えられていたことは君も知ってるだろう。幸か不幸か，わしはそれを操る方法を身に付けてしまったんだよ。

クリントン: 本当ですか？ どうやってそれに気づいたんです？

バーンハウス: 今から10年ほど前，1948年のことだ。よせばいいのに心理学会に出席してな。あまり人づき合いが悪いと思われてもいかんので，サイコロゲームに参加してみた。後にも先にもその時だけだよ。

          my life — in a dice game.

Clint: What happened?

Barn: I didn't have the faintest idea what was expected of me. And someone told me to roll sevens. So, I did — ten of them.

Clint: I bet you weren't asked back into that game.

Barn: That night, in my room, I realized that it simply couldn't have been an accident, Clinton. I tried to reconstruct the exact scene — the position of my body — and finally, the thoughts in my mind. And that was what did it. I remembered what had been my train of thought and I proceeded to roll sevens; not ten consecutive times, but fifty. (*rolls dice*)

Clint: Brother, there it is again. Professor, can you do anything else? I mean, besides shove dice around?

Barn: You see that inkwell on my desk?

Clint: Sure.

クリントン: 　で，どうなりましたか？

バーンハウス: 　何をどうしたらよいか見当もつかなかったが，誰かが 7 を出せというんでな，7 を出した。10 回もさ。

クリントン: 　もう誰も教授をサイコロゲームに誘ってくれなくなったでしょうね。

バーンハウス: 　その夜，わしは部屋で考えた。これは決して偶然ではあり得ない，とね。わしはその時の様子を正確に再現してみようと試みた。その時の自分の姿勢，そしてついには何を考えていたかも再現してみた。まさにそれが正解だった。自分の考えの連鎖を思い出しながらサイコロを振ってみると，7 が出た。それも 10 回連続ではなく，50 回連続でな。（サイコロを振る）

クリントン: 　なんと，また 7 ですよ！　教授，ほかにできることはないんですか，サイコロを動かす以外に。

バーンハウス: 　デスクの上にインク瓶があるね。

クリントン: 　ええ。

Barn: Watch it. Don't take your eyes off it. If nothing happens, say so, and I shall go quietly — even happily — to the nearest sanitorium.

Clint: Okay, Professor, shoot. (*inkwell shatters*) Hey! Why, it just blew up!

Barn: Yes. I'm sorry. I didn't mean to splash ink on your suit.

Clint: Why, why, that's okay, Professor. What was that funny noise?

Barn: Oh, that? The dynamo psychic waves are a little like ultra-high frequency waves. Sometimes when I turn on the power, they create a kind of static.

Clint: Listen, Professor, how much power have you got? Could you blow up anything... well, you know — big?

Barn: I could threaten the Great Wall of China.

Clint: Oh, you'll make the helio-oxygen bomb look sick!

バーンハウス： 　見ててごらん。目を離さないように。もし何も起こらなければそう言ってくれ，わしは文句も言わずに喜んで近くの精神病院へ入院するから。

クリントン： 　じゃあ教授，はじめてください。（インク瓶が砕け散る）うわっ，破裂しましたよ！

バーンハウス： 　うむ。おっと申し訳ない，君の背広をインクで汚してしまったようだな。

クリントン： 　いや，別に構いません，教授。でもあの妙な音は何だったんですか？

バーンハウス： 　あれかね？ 念動波はちょっと超高周波に似ていて，わしがそのパワーを使おうとすると，時には一種の雑音を発するんだよ。

クリントン： 　それで教授，パワーはどのくらいあるんです？ 何かもっと大きなものも破壊できるんですか？

バーンハウス： 　中国の万里の長城も壊せるだろうな。

クリントン： 　ヘリオ酸素爆弾もまっさおじゃないですか。

Barn: That's what scares me, Clinton. The thought that maybe I could use this power to save the world. Clinton, you've got to help me!

Clint: Who, me? Professor, when it comes to international relations, I don't know from where. You'd better get in touch with the State Department.

Barn: State Department. Yes, they'd be the ones, wouldn't they? Well, you probably want to be getting home now. I'll see you to the door. I could use a breath of fresh air.

Clint: Okay, Professor.... You'd better stop brooding about this. You get somebody else to do your worrying for you.

Barn: Yes, yes, you're right. I have been brooding, wondering what to do. Just sitting and staring endlessly at that awful monstrosity across the way.

Clint: You mean the old bell tower?

バーンハウス：	怖じ気づいたのはその点さ，クリントン君。このパワーを使えばわしは世界を救えるかもしれん，とは思うんだが。クリントン君，ひとつわしに力を貸してくれんか。
クリントン：	私ですか？ でも教授，国際関係は私もさっぱりですからね。国務省に連絡されたほうがいいんじゃありませんか。
バーンハウス：	国務省か。確かに彼らの管轄かもしれんな。さてと，君ももう帰宅したくなったろう。戸口まで送ってあげるよ。わしも少し外の空気を吸いたいしな。
クリントン：	すみませんね，教授。あまり考え込むのはやめたほうがいいですよ。誰かほかの人に悩んでもらったらどうです。
バーンハウス：	わかった，わかった，君の言うとおりにしよう。確かに考え込み過ぎたかもしれんな，どうしたらよいかわからずに。ただじっと座って，いつまでも向かいの醜い建物を眺めていても仕方のないことだ。
クリントン：	あの古い鐘楼(しょうろう)のことですか？

Barn: Yes. I've gotten so I can't stand the sight of it any more. (*sound of explosion*)

Clint: Professor! Professor, look! Why, there's nothing left but a pile of rubble.

Barn: Oh, my. I didn't really mean to do that. So you see, Clinton, it's got to the point where my lightest whim is more dangerous than a blockbuster.

Clint: Professor, you'd better write that letter to the State Department right now. You pack too much of a wallop. (*music*)

バーンハウス: そうだ。もう飽き飽きして見るのも嫌だ。（爆発音）

クリントン: 教授，教授，ご覧なさい！ 瓦礫(がれき)の山になってしまいましたよ！

バーンハウス: なんてことだ。そんなつもりなどなかったのに。クリントン君，これでわかったろう。今じゃわしのほんの気まぐれは大型爆弾より危険なんだ。

クリントン: 教授，今すぐ国務省に手紙を書いたほうがいいですよ。教授のパワーは凄すぎます。　　　　　　　　　　　　（音楽）

2

Clint: Professor Barnhouse mailed his letter, and things happened fast. The long arm of the army reached out, and within five days, the two of us were deposited in an old mansion in Virginia, surrounded with a barbed wire fence and twenty guards and labelled "Top Secret." As soon as they'd seen a couple of small demonstrations, they set up a big test of dynamo psychism, and the professor was a very important guy. You could see him getting more unhappy every day.

Barn: General Barker, I've got to talk to you.

Barker: Just a minute, Professor. We're cleaning up the last details on Operation Brain waves. We'll roll at 14:00 hours tomorrow.

Barn: At 14:00 what?

Barke: Two o'clock tomorrow afternoon. Robot control fighter rockets will take

⑵

クリントン： 　バーンハウス教授が手紙を出すと，その後の展開は急だった。陸軍が周到に手を回し，５日と経たないうちに私たち２人はバージニア州にある古い邸宅へと連れて行かれた。その周囲は鉄条網と20人の警備兵で守られ，「極秘」の文字が掲げられていた。軍関係者に簡単な実証を２つほどやってみせると，彼らはすぐさま大がかりな念動実験を行うことを決め，教授はたちまち重要人物となった。しかし教授は毎日目に見えて不機嫌になっていった。

バーンハウス： バーカー将軍，話したいことがあるんだが。
バーカー： 　少々お待ち願えますか，教授。「脳波作戦」の最終調整をしているところでしてな。決行は明日の 14:00 時です。

バーンハウス： 14:00 時？ 何のことかね？
バーカー： 　明日午後２時のことですよ。ロボット操縦のロケット戦闘機が 14:00 時のきっかり 10 分前に出撃し，目標上空に 14:

off at exactly 14:00 minus ten and appear over the target at 14:00. Watching from here over the video screen, you will then try to knock all twenty of them out of the sky. Think you can do it?

Barn: Of course, I can do it, but...

Barke: Fine. Then we've taken care of everything.

Barn: Everything — except that you neglected to ask me if I wanted to do it. I don't. This whole thing strikes me as childish and insanely expensive.

Barke: *We'll* decide about that.

Barn: But what's the good of it? I wouldn't mind acting as a defense weapon if it were necessary. But I can make all wars and armaments unnecessary. I could give every nation what it needs. I could move mountains, build roads, dig irrigation canals. I have a technique which costs nothing and could do immense good.

　　　　　　　　00 時に到着します。あなたはここからテレビ画面でそれを
　　　　　　　　確認して，20 機全部を撃墜するんです。できますか？

バーンハウス：　そりゃできるとも。だが……。
バーカー：　　　よろしい。では準備万端です。

バーンハウス：　　準備万端？ ひとつ忘れておらんかね，わしの意向を尋ね
　　　　　　　　ることを。わしは嫌だ。だいたいこの計画は子供じみとるし，
　　　　　　　　費用だってばかにならん。

バーカー：　　　それは我々が判断することです。
バーンハウス：　　そもそも何の役に立つというのかね？ 必要とあればわし
　　　　　　　　も自衛のための武器になってもよいとは思っとる。しかし，
　　　　　　　　わしは戦争も武装の必要もなくせるんだよ。あらゆる国の望
　　　　　　　　みをかなえることができるんだ。山をどかし，道路を作り，
　　　　　　　　用水路も掘ってやれる。わしのやり方は一銭もかからず，し
　　　　　　　　かも大いに人のためになるんだ。なのに君たちは何百万ドル
　　　　　　　　もかけて，その強大な破壊力ばかりを証明しようと躍起にな
　　　　　　　　っておる。無意味だとは思わんかね。

You're spending millions to prove that it can do immense damage. It doesn't make sense.

Clint: You know something, General, he's right.

Barn: Of course I'm right. I want you to send me and Clinton back to Wilton College. Right away.

Barke: That's quite impossible, Professor. This operation has gone too far to be called off now.

Barn: Yes, but...

Barke: Even if we wanted to call it off. If your dynamo psychism really works, you're apt to be the key to our entire defense effort.

Barn: But, listen...

Barke: You'll have to excuse me now. Major Guthro and I have to double-check the confidential list of the observers on this end. Have you got it, Major?

Guth: Yes, General, it's right here. Alberts,

クリントン: 将軍，教授の言うとおりですよ。

バーンハウス: そうだとも。わしとクリントン君をウィルトン大学に連れ戻してくれたまえ。すぐにだ。

バーカー: それは無理ですな，教授。作戦はもう後戻りできないところまで来ているんです。

バーンハウス: そうかもしれんが……。

バーカー: 中止したくてももう手遅れです。あなたの念動力の効果が実証されれば，あなたは国防システム全体の要となるんですから。

バーンハウス: ちょっと待ってくれ……。

バーカー: これで失礼させていただきますよ。ガスロ少佐と私はこちらに参加するオブザーバーの極秘リストをダブルチェックしなければなりませんのでね。少佐，リストは持ったか？

ガスロ: はい，将軍，ここにあります。アルバーツ，バーカー，バ

	Barker, Bernstein, Carter, Clinton, Guthro, Hollbrook, Lawrence, Stein, Williams, sir.
Barke:	Check. I guess that includes everybody of importance.
Barn:	What about me?
Barke:	What? Oh, that's taken for granted, Professor.
Barn:	Thanks.
Barke:	14:00 hours. Will you be ready?
Barn:	I'll be ready. And now if someone will wind the restricted clock and put the confidential cat out, I'm going to bed.

(*music*)

ーンスタイン，カーター，クリントン，ガスロ，ホルブルック，ローレンス，スタイン，ウィリアムズ，以上です。

バーカー：　よし。これで重要人物は全員だな。

バーンハウス：　わしは仲間はずれかね？
バーカー：　何ですと？　ああ，もちろん教授は言わずとも入っています。

バーンハウス：　そうかな。
バーカー：　14:00 時ですからな。準備をよろしく。
バーンハウス：　わかっとる。誰か「極秘」に目覚ましをかけて，「極秘」に寝支度をしてもらおうか，わしはもう床に就くからな。

（音楽）

3

McKinley: (*radar beeps start*) YDR to Brainwave Control. Observation plane to Brainwave Control. Come in, please.

Barke: That's McKinley, in the observation plane. Cut me in. Hello, McKinley. Reading you clear on the speaker. Everything all right?

McK: All okay, General. Take-off uneventful. Fighter rockets now flying on course in perfect formation. Altitude, 5,000 feet. Air speed — 865. Visibility unlimited. Are you tracking us?

Barke: We've got you on radar. Haven't picked you up on the video screen yet. What's your estimated time of arrival over the target?

McK: ETA — two minutes.

Barke: Check. Remember, McKinley. The

⑶

マッキンリー： 　（レーダーの電子音）ＹＤＲから脳波作戦司令部。観察機から脳波作戦司令部。応答願います。

バーカー： 　観察機のマッキンリーからだ。私につないでくれ。もしもし，マッキンリー，そちらの声はスピーカーからよく聞こえるぞ。すべて順調か？

マッキンリー： 　すべて順調です，将軍。離陸は異常なし。ロケット戦闘機は編隊を崩さずコースを飛行中。高度5,000フィート。速度865。視界きわめて良好。本機の追尾状況はどうでしょうか。

バーカー： 　レーダーに映っている。テレビ画面にはまだ姿が見えない。目標への推定到着時刻は？

マッキンリー： 　推定到着時刻2分です。
バーカー： 　よし。いいか，マッキンリー，観察機は目標エリアに入る

observation plane is not to enter the target range. Veer off and circle at the ten-mile limit. Bring the rockets overhead by remote control.

McK: Check. Observation signing off.

Barke: One minute, 45 seconds to go, Professor Barnhouse. Are you in good shape?

Barn: I'm all right, General.

Barke: Good. We can all take our places in front of the video screen now. You sit here, Professor... Major Guthro, will you turn on the video screen?

Guth: Right, General. Nothing yet; just empty sky. Hold it, I hear them coming in. (*sound of aircraft*)

Barke: There are twenty of them, Professor. Do you think you can knock them down at this altitude?

Barn: Distance has nothing to do with it.

Barke: I don't want anything to go wrong.

なよ。横にそれて，10マイル離れて旋回するんだ。ロケットは遠隔操作で上空に誘導しろ。

マッキンリー： 了解。観察機，以上。
バーカー： あと1分45秒です，バーンハウス教授，調子はどうです。

バーンハウス： 大丈夫だよ，将軍。
バーカー： よろしい。では，全員テレビ画面前の定位置に着くように。教授，こちらにお座りください。ガスロ少佐，テレビ画面のスイッチを入れてくれたまえ。

ガスロ： 了解です，将軍。まだ何も映っていません。空だけです。あ，近づいてくる音がします。（飛行機の音）

バーカー： 20機ありますよ，教授。この高度で全部撃墜できますか？

バーンハウス： 距離は関係ない。
バーカー： 少しの失敗も許されないんです。本当に大丈夫ですか？

	You're sure you feel all right?
Barn:	General, I know I can do it. If that's all that's worrying you, let's call the whole thing off and save 20 million dollars.
Guth:	There they are. They're coming in.
Barke:	Get ready, Professor. Ten seconds, nine, eight, seven, six, five, four, three, two, one. Now! Wide open, Professor! (*Radar beep stops*)
Barke:	Well, go ahead, Barnhouse, knock them down!
Barn:	I did. (*sound of plane*)
Barke:	Nonsense. All you've done is black out the video screen. What went wrong? Did you give it everything you had?
Barn:	I was wide open, General.
Barke:	But it didn't work. They're still flying, they're... (*explosion*) What's that?
Barn:	It just took a few seconds to work. (*explosion*)
Barke:	Holy smoke! They're dropping like

バーンハウス:	絶対にできるとも。できるかどうかだけを心配しているなら，この実験はもう終わりにして2,000万ドルのムダ遣いをやめようじゃないか。
ガスロ:	来ました。接近しています。
バーカー:	準備願いますよ，教授。10秒，9秒，8，7，6，5，4，3，2，1。今だ，行け，教授！（レーダー音止まる）
バーカー:	どうした，やるんだ，バーンハウス，撃ち落とせ！
バーンハウス:	もう済んだよ。（飛行機の音）
バーカー:	ばかな。テレビ画面が消えただけじゃないか。何がいけなかったんだ？ 本気を出したんだろうな？
バーンハウス:	全力でやったさ，将軍。
バーカー:	だが失敗だ。まだ飛び続けているじゃないか，まるで…（爆発音）何だ，今のは？
バーンハウス:	効果が出るまでに数秒かかったんだ。（爆発音）
バーカー:	こりゃ驚いた，ハエみたいに落ちて行く！

flies.

McK: McKinley to Brainwave Control! Look what's happened to these rockets? They're going down in flames.

Barke: By Heaven! It works. It really works!... Get Washington on the line! Barnhouse, I want you to... Hey! Hey, where's Barnhouse? Clinton, where's the professor?

Clint: Got me, General. We were all staring at the video. He must have walked out.

Barke: Get moving, everybody. Alert the guards! Search the house! If anything happens to that man...

Corporal: General Barker, General Barker! (*siren*)

Barke: What is it, Corporal?

Corp: Corporal Gray, guard at the main gate. Sir, Professor Barnhouse has gone.

Barke: Gone? Where?

Corp: He came tearing out of the gate at forty miles an hour. Here's a note, sir. He

マッキンリー： 　マッキンリーから脳波作戦司令部！　ご覧になりましたか，ロケットの様子を？　炎上して墜落しています。

バーカー： 　なんと，成功だ，こいつは使えるぞ！　ワシントンに電話をつなげ！　バーンハウス，君には……おい，バーンハウスはどこへ行った？　クリントン，教授はどこだ？

クリントン： 　私も知りません，将軍。みんなテレビ画面を見つめてましたから，きっとその間に出て行ったんでしょう。

バーカー： 　みんな，ぼーっとしてないで捜せ！　警護兵に知らせろ！　建物の中をくまなく捜すんだ！　あの男に万一のことがあったら…

伍長： 　バーカー将軍，バーカー将軍！（サイレン音）

バーカー： 　何だ，伍長？

伍長： 　正門を警護しているグレイ伍長です。バーンハウス教授が逃走しました。

バーカー： 　逃走？　どこへ？

伍長： 　正門を時速40マイルで突っ切って行きました。メモがあります。車で通り過ぎる時に教授が投げ捨てて行ったんです。

	threw it out of the car as he went by. I picked it up.
Barke:	Let me see it, quick. What the... What got into that man?
Clint:	What does he say, General?
Barke:	"Gentlemen, as the first super weapon with a conscience, I am removing myself from your national defense stockpile. Setting a new precedent in the behavior of ordinance, I have humane reasons for going off." Signed, "Arthur Barnhouse."

(*siren ends*)

私が拾いました。

バーカー： ぐずぐずせずに見せろ。いったい全体……どうしたっていうんだ，あの男は。

クリントン： 何と書いてあるんです，将軍。

バーカー： 「諸君。私は良心を持った最初のスーパー兵器として，国防兵器庫からの離脱を選んだ。兵器の行動としては前例のないことだが，私は道義的な理由からあえて失踪する」署名：「アーサー・バーンハウス」。（サイレン音が止む）

4

Clint: Barnhouse was gone, and within twelve hours the world was on a spree. The headlines were glorious or terrible, depending on what you think of the things the way they are.

Newsboy: **A.R. Barnhouse whacks through helio bomb factory.**

Clint: The dynamo psychic waves reached every corner of the world; and every country — every continent — flashed the news of what was happening.

News: **A. R. Barnhouse knocks out hidden atomic stockpile in Asia.**

Clint: There was a new kind of war — the war of tattletales. Secret agents of every country hunted for the hidden armaments of their

(4)

クリントン： 　バーンハウス教授が去って半日も経たないうちに，世間は騒然となった。紙面に踊る見出しに万歳を叫ぶか脅威を感じるかは，読む人によってさまざまだった。

新聞売の少年： 　A. R. バーンハウスがヘリオ爆弾工場を破壊！

クリントン： 　念動波の威力は世界の隅々にまで到達し，全大陸のあらゆる国がそのニュースで持ちきりとなった。

新聞売の少年： 　A. R. バーンハウスがアジアに密かに備蓄されていた原子力兵器を撃滅！

クリントン： 　新しい戦争が始まっていた。告げ口戦争だ。各国の諜報員は，敵国が隠している軍備を探し出し，これを新聞で大々的

enemies. Yelled about them in the newspapers. And immediately, there'd be that warning burst of Barnhouse static, followed by...

News: Radio-control fleet blown up on secret maneuver.

Clint: The professor was out to make peace or bust. And nothing like him ever was.

5

Clint: Look, Major Guthro, I told the FBI and the army everything I know, weeks ago. I've answered questions 'til I'm blue in the face.

Guth: I didn't come here to ask questions, Clinton. I came to ask for your help.

Clint: *My* help?

Guth: That's right. To find Barnhouse.

Clint: What if I don't want to?

に報じた。するとたちまちバーンハウス念動波の予兆の雑音が聞こえ，次いで……。

新聞売の少年： 極秘任務中の無線操縦艦隊が爆発！

クリントン： 教授は必死で平和を築こうとしていたのだ。彼のような存在はまさに前代未聞だった。

(5)

クリントン： ガスロ少佐，僕はＦＢＩにも軍にも知っていることはすべて話しましたよ，何週間も前に。質問にはすべて洗いざらい答えましたからね。

ガスロ： いや，質問をしに来たんじゃないんだ，クリントン君。手伝ってほしいんだよ。

クリントン： 私に？

ガスロ： そうだ。バーンハウスの捜索をね。

クリントン： 嫌だと言ったら？

Guth: If you're his friend, I think you'd better.

Clint: Why pick on me? You've got the FBI, the police, and Army Intelligence; why can't you find him yourselves?

Guth: We're trying. But you know the man well. You could spot him where we wouldn't. You're the only one who can.

Clint: Maybe. But why should I? Wherever he is, I think he's doing fine. He's making war impossible, and I like it.

Guth: So do I.

Clint: Yes? He's putting you out of a job.

Guth: That's all right with me. I'll retire to a truck farm with pleasure.

Clint: Well, then?

Guth: Look, Clinton. We aren't the only ones in this race. Every country in the world has its best agents out hunting for Barnhouse. Nobody can beat that kind of a manhunt.

ガスロ： 友だちなら助けてやるべきじゃないのか？

クリントン： なぜ僕に？ ＦＢＩや警察や，軍の諜報機関だってあるじゃないですか。自力で捜せないんですか？

ガスロ： 努力はしてるさ。しかし君は教授をよく知ってる。我々の思いもよらない場所にいる教授を，君なら捜し当てられるはずだ。

クリントン： そうかもしれませんが，手伝う理由がないでしょう。教授は今どこにいようと大丈夫だと思いますよ。彼は戦争を不可能にしようとしているんだ。実にいいことです。

ガスロ： 私もそう思う。

クリントン： ほんとですか？ あなたの仕事がなくなるんですよ。

ガスロ： 私はそれでも構わんさ。喜んで引退して畑でも耕すよ。

クリントン： じゃ，ほっとけばいいでしょう。

ガスロ： いいか，クリントン君，競争に参加してるのは我が国だけじゃないんだぞ。世界各国が腕利きの諜報員を注ぎ込んでバーンハウスを捜してるんだ。誰だろうともう逃げきれんよ。

Clint: He seems to be doing all right so far.

Guth: Sure. But how long do you think he can keep it up? A week? A month? Sooner or later, he'll be spotted. And if the wrong people find him, Clinton, we're done for. You know what kind of weapon this is. Whoever controls the Barnhouse Effect will control the world.

Clint: All right. Suppose they do find him? He'd never give the secret away.

Guth: Never give it away! Are you out of your mind? Do you think these fellows are playing for marbles?

Clint: Well, no, I...

Guth: Read the papers, Clinton. Don't you know what's going on in the rest of the world?

Clint: Yes, I...

Guth: They'll get the secret out of Barnhouse, all right. What happens to him in the process won't be very pretty.

クリントン： でも現に教授は無事じゃないですか。
ガスロ： 今のところはな。しかしいつまで逃げ続けられると思う？1週間，それとも1か月？ いずれ見つかるよ。もし悪い相手につかまったらおしまいだぞ，クリントン君。これがどんなに凄い兵器かは君も知ってるだろう。バーンハウス効果を制するものは世界を制するんだ。

クリントン： 仮に教授が彼らに見つかったとしても，教授は絶対に秘密を明かしたりはしませんよ。
ガスロ： 絶対に明かさないだって？ 本気でそう思ってるのか？ 相手はお遊びじゃない，真剣なんだぞ。

クリントン： そりゃそうでしょうけれど……。
ガスロ： 新聞を読んでみるがいい。世界で何が起きているか知らないのか？

クリントン： 知ってますが……。
ガスロ： 奴らは間違いなくバーンハウスから秘密を聞き出すさ。ただ，聞き出す過程で教授の身に何が起きるかは考えたくもないがね。

Clint: Well, he... he must realize that, then. He'll never let himself be taken alive.

Guth: He may not have the choice. And if he doesn't, God help us all.

Clint: All right. All right, I'm in.

Guth: Good. Now, do you know anything that you haven't told us? Anything that might give us a lead?

Clint: Only this. (*sound of paper*) It was addressed to me. I found it here on his desk the morning after he escaped.

Guth: You mean he came back here?

Clint: Yes. I guess he needed to pick up some personal effects. Anyway, the files were open, and he left this note on a scrap of paper.

Guth: Anything to do with the Barnhouse Effect?

Clint: Read it yourself. It's Greek to me. Just these few lines scrawled on a piece of paper, and the last one breaks off right in

クリントン：	でも，教授もそのくらいはわかっているはずです。生きてつかまったりはしないでしょう。
ガスロ：	有無を言わさず連れ去られるかもしれんじゃないか。そうなったら我々はおしまいだよ。
クリントン：	わかりました，手伝いましょう。
ガスロ：	よかろう。で，我々にまだ話していないことはないかね？何か手がかりになりそうなことは。
クリントン：	これだけです。（紙がすれる音）僕宛のメモです。教授が逃げた翌朝に，教授のデスクに置かれていたんです。
ガスロ：	じゃ，教授はここへ戻ってきたのか？
クリントン：	そうです。たぶん身の回りの物を取りに来たんでしょう。書類戸棚が開いていて，それから紙切れに書かれたこのメモが残っていたんです。
ガスロ：	バーンハウス効果と関係のある内容かね？
クリントン：	ご自分で読んでみてください。私には意味不明です。紙切れに数行なぐり書きがあるだけで，最後の行は文の途中で切れています。

Guth: the middle of a sentence.

Hm. This stuff doesn't make any sense at all. You know, from the looks of this, I'm beginning to wonder if the professor isn't going off his rocker.

Clint: I thought of that, too.

Guth: All the more reason why we've got to get to him — quick. He may be helpless, and the whole world's on his track. C'mon, Clinton, we haven't much time.

6

Guth: You say you do recognize this photograph, Mrs. Reardon?

Reardon: I tell you, it looks like Mr. Balford. He had the second-floor sunroom for quite a while, but he left — oh, I should say — about a week ago. Say, is he wanted for something?

Guth: Yes, if he's the man I think he is.

ガスロ：　ふん。こりゃさっぱり意味をなさんな。この様子から察すると，教授は気が狂ったとしか思えんが。

クリントン：　僕もそう思いました。
ガスロ：　じゃあなおさら急いで教授を捜さんとな。困ってるかもしれん。世界中が教授を追ってるしな。さあ早く，クリントン君，時間がないんだ。

(6)

ガスロ：　リアドンさん，この写真の人物に見覚えがあるんですね？

リアドン：　ええ，バルフォードさんに似てますわ。２階のサンルームに長い間滞在してたんですが，お発ちになりましたよ。えーと，１週間ぐらい前でしょうか。あの方，指名手配中なんですか？

ガスロ：　ええ，もし我々が考えている人物ならね。

Rear: Well, now, I'd say you're looking for the wrong fella. That Mr. Balford, he couldn't be a criminal. Why, he wouldn't even harm a fly. He spent all his time in his room — just thinkin'.

7

Corp: Oh, brother, it's hot. What a way to spend an August afternoon, huh, Major? Give my eyeteeth to be at Jones Beach.

Guth: So would I, Corporal, but we've got work to do here.

Corp: Look, sir, we've been cruising around in these radio detection cars for a week. Not a sign of Barnhouse static. The professor must have run out of things to work on.

Guth: Well, we'll give it a little more time. Switch to shortwave; see if there's anything special coming through.

リアドン： あら，きっと人違いよ。バルフォードさんは犯罪者なんかじゃないわ。虫も殺せないような方ですもの。一日中お部屋にこもって，じっと考えごとをしてらっしゃったわ。

(7)

伍長： 参ったな，なんて暑さだ。8月の昼下がりをこんなふうに過ごすなんて，かなわんですな，少佐。できるもんならジョーンズビーチで過ごしたかったところですよ。

ガスロ： 同感だ，伍長，だが仕事だからな。

伍長： 少佐，無線探査装置を積んだこの車でもう1週間も探索してますが，バーンハウス効果の音はさっぱり聞こえませんよ。教授がやっつける対象はもう全滅しちまったんじゃないですか。

ガスロ： まあ，もう少し続けてみようじゃないか。短波に切り替えてみてくれ。何か変わったニュースがあるかもしれん。

Corp:	Yes, sir.
Guth:	(*radio signals*) Try the 900 wave. Let's hear that.
Radio:	Our American enemies, who have hidden behind the unjust and diabolical persecution by Professor Arthur Barnhouse...
Corp:	Uh, oh...
Radio:	... will tyrannize us no more.
Corp:	I wonder if the professor's on this?
Radio:	Anyhow, our glorious leader takes up his residence in a shelter, sealed up with lead against all dynamo psychic rays. This is protection designed by our brilliant scientists to be absolutely impregnable against the Barnhouse Effect. He will once again lead us on the path of our glorious destiny...
	(*sound of dynamo psychic waves*)
Guth:	Quick, try it 'til you get me a fix.
Corp:	(*beep*) I got it. Let me check this chart.

伍長：	了解。
ガスロ：	（ラジオ信号）900に合わせてくれ。聞いてみよう。
ラジオ：	敵国アメリカが隠れて行っている不正かつ極悪非道の迫害は，アーサー・バーンハウス教授によるものだが……。
伍長：	おっと……。
ラジオ：	……我が国への脅威は終わりを告げるだろう。
伍長：	教授はこれを聞いているでしょうかね……。
ラジオ：	我が国の栄光ある指導者は，一切の念動波を遮断する鉛のシェルターの中に住まいを移した。この防護は，バーンハウス効果から絶対に被害を受けないよう我が国の優秀な科学者たちが設計したものだ。我が国の指導者は，再び国民をその輝かしい運命へと導くであろう……。
	（念動波の音）
ガスロ：	急げ，発信源を特定するんだ。
伍長：	（電子音）捕捉しました。チャートで確認します。

Guth: Quick, man!

Corp: Two point nine, one point seven. Oh, my aching back!

Guth: What is it?

Corp: We haven't got a prayer of finding him, Major. He has to be picked out of two million people.

Guth: Where is Barnhouse?

Corp: Right where I was wishing I was. Right smack in the middle of Jones Beach.

8

Hotelman: (*front desk bell*) Sorry, gents, we're full. No more rooms tonight.

Guth: We don't want a room. Do you recognize this picture?

Hotel: Who wants to know?

Guth: Uncle wants to know.

Hotel: Oh, oh, excuse me. I'm sorry. Here, let

ガスロ：　　　　　ぐずぐずするな！

伍長：　　　　　2.9, 1.7, あっ, なんてこった！

ガスロ：　　　　　どうした？

伍長：　　　　　見つけるのはまず不可能です, 少佐。200万人もの中から探すなんて。

ガスロ：　　　　　どこにいるんだ, バーンハウスは？

伍長：　　　　　さっき私が行きたいと言っていたところです。ジョーンズビーチのまっただ中ですよ。

⑻

ホテル従業員：　　（フロントのベル音）だめだよ, 今夜は満室で空きがないんだ。

ガスロ：　　　　　宿泊じゃない。この写真の人物に見覚えはないか？

ホテル従業員：　　誰だい, あんた？

ガスロ：　　　　　政府の者だ。

ホテル従業員：　　おっと, こりゃ失礼。見せてもらおうか？ ええと……そ

	me see it. I... yeah... yeah, it looks a lot like room four seventeen.
Guth:	About five feet eight, thin, sandy hair, glasses, little scar right across the bridge of his nose?
Hotel:	Yes, that's four seventeen, all right.
Guth:	You mean he's here now?
Hotel:	No, not any more. He checked out two days ago. But he couldn't have gone far.
Guth:	What makes you say that?
Hotel:	Well, he looked sick as a dog. Couldn't hardly carry his own bag up.
Guth:	Uh, oh.
Hotel:	Like I said to the other fellas. I said, "He looked like he was on his way to a morgue."
Guth:	What other fellows?
Hotel:	Heh? Oh, the ones this morning. You're the second pair that's been asking for him. (*music*)

うだな，417号室の客によく似てるな。

ガスロ： 背丈は5フィート8インチぐらい，やせ形で白髪まじり，眼鏡をかけていて，鼻筋を横切るような小さな傷跡があるんだが。

ホテル従業員： まさに417号室の客だね。
ガスロ： 今滞在してるのか？
ホテル従業員： いや，もう発ったよ，2日前に。でもそう遠くへ行っちゃいないと思うけどね。
ガスロ： なぜそう思うのかね。
ホテル従業員： ひどく具合が悪そうで，自分の荷物を持ち上げるのもやっとだったからね。
ガスロ： それはいかんな。
ホテル従業員： 別の連中にも言ったんだ。「そのまま死体安置所に行くんじゃないかと思ったくらいだ」ってね。

ガスロ： 別の連中って？
ホテル従業員： え？ 今朝の連中さ。こいつを捜しに来たのはあんた方で2組目なんだよ。　　　　　　　　　　　　　　　（音楽）

9

Nurse: *(footsteps)* Here we are. Ward fifteen. This way, gentlemen.

Guth: You're sure he's here, Nurse?

Nur: Oh, yes.

Guth: Thank Heavens, we're in time.

Nur: Well, I wasn't on duty when he came in, but one of the other girls told me he'd collapsed in the street. The ambulance brought him in.

Guth: Poor guy, he must have really had it rough.

Nur: Oh, here you are. Bed number 78. This is your man.

Guth: Wait a minute. This isn't Barnhouse!

Nur: But, I was perfectly sure. Wait, let me check his chart. "Dismissed, 8 p.m."

Guth: Only an hour ago.

Nur: Oh, dear. Now I remember.

⑼

看護師：	（足音）ここですわ。第 15 病棟。こちらへどうぞ。
ガスロ：	彼は本当にここにいるんだね？
看護師：	ええ。
ガスロ：	よかった，間に合ったぞ。
看護師：	あの方が入院された時，私は当直ではなかったんですが，別の看護師によれば行き倒れだったそうです。救急車で運び込まれたんです。
ガスロ：	気の毒に，さぞ大変だったろう。
看護師：	ああ，こちらです。78 番ベッド。これがお捜しの方です。
ガスロ：	ちょっと待て，これはバーンハウスじゃない！
看護師：	えっ？ 絶対に間違いないと思ったんですけど。そうだ，診療記録を見ればわかります……「午後 8 時，退院」
ガスロ：	つい 1 時間前だ。
看護師：	あらいけない，今思い出したわ。

Guth: Remember what? If he was sick, why did you let him go?

Nur: Well, two of his friends came and took him away. They didn't want him in the charity ward. They said they'd make sure that he was taken care of. (*music*)

10

Clint: (*door opens*) Every time I walk into this study, I keep hoping somehow I'll wake up out of a bad dream and find the professor just sitting here. Major, is there anything we haven't covered?

Guth: Nothing. The police, the FBI, the air patrol, the docks, the railroad stations, everything. Not even a flea could get through this dragnet — I hope.

Clint: Then, I guess we sit. We sit! Maybe something will come in. (*rolls dice*)

Guth: Do you have to roll those dice?

ガスロ： 思い出したって，何を？ 病人なのになぜ退院させたんだ？

看護師： お友だち2人がやって来て連れて行かれたんです。無料病棟には置いておけない，自分たちがちゃんと面倒を見させるからって。　　　　　　　　　　　　　　　　　　（音楽）

(10)

クリントン： （ドアの開く音）この研究室に入る度に，悪夢がさめて教授がそこに座っていることを願わずにはいられないんです。何か手を打ち忘れてはいないでしょうか，少佐。

ガスロ： いや。警察，FBI，航空パトロール，港湾，鉄道など，すべて手は尽くした。もうねずみ1匹逃げられない——と思いたいところだ。

クリントン： それじゃ，もう待つしかありませんね。腰を落ち着けて，何かが起きるのを待つとしましょうか。（サイコロを振る）

ガスロ： 君，サイコロをころがすのはやめてくれんかね。

Clint: I'm sorry. I'm sorry. I wasn't thinking.

Guth: An hour. That's what's driving me crazy. One hour sooner and he'd have been in our hands, not theirs.

Clint: I know. Well, maybe he's still all right.

Guth: How can he be all right? He's in the hands of a foreign power.

Clint: We don't know that for sure. The professor was a likeable enough guy. He couldn't have lasted this long if he hadn't found some friends. Maybe they came and took him away.

Guth: Well, I... *(phone rings)* Grab that.

Clint: Hello. Yes?

Barn: Clinton, is that you?

Clint: Professor Barnhouse.

Barn: Clinton, they've got me.

Clint: Who's got you? Where are you, Professor?

Barn: I don't know. They said something about taking me to an airport.

クリントン:	すみません，ぼーっとしてしまって。	
ガスロ:	たった１時間差。それが悔しくてならん。１時間前に行っていれば，奴らではなく我々の手に渡っていたのに。	
クリントン:	そうですね。でも，教授は無事かもしれませんよ。	
ガスロ:	無事なわけがないだろう。外国政府に連れ去られたんだぞ。	
クリントン:	でも確証はないでしょう。教授は人に好かれるタイプですし，それに誰か友だちを作らなければ今まで隠れ続けるのは無理です。きっと協力者が来て連れて行ったんですよ。	
ガスロ:	だといいが……（電話が鳴る）出てくれんか。	
クリントン:	もしもし。どなたですか。	
バーンハウス:	クリントン君，君か？	
クリントン:	バーンハウス教授。	
バーンハウス:	クリントン君，つかまったよ。	
クリントン:	つかまったって，誰にです？ 今どこですか，教授？	
バーンハウス:	わからん。奴らはわしを空港に連れて行くとか言っておった。	

Clint:		An airport? Which one?
Barn:		Listen, Clinton. I've got to tell you. The inkwell.
Clint:		What are you talking about?
Barn:		Remember, the ink... aggrh... (*phone is hung up*)
Clint:		Professor! Professor Barnhouse!... Operator. Operator!
Operator:		Your call, please?
Clint:		Operator, that call that just came in here. Can you trace it?
Ope:		I'm sorry, sir, but I'm afraid it's too late. Your party has been disconnected.

(*music*)

クリントン：	空港？　どの空港です？
バーンハウス：	よく聞くんだ，クリントン君。言いたいことがある。インク瓶だ。
クリントン：	何のことですか？
バーンハウス：	忘れるなよ。インク……うわーっ（電話切れる）
クリントン：	教授！　バーンハウス教授！……交換手，交換手！
交換手：	どちらへおつなぎしましょうか。
クリントン：	交換手，今ここにかかってきた電話だが，逆探知できるか？
交換手：	申し訳ありませんが，もう手遅れです。先方が電話を切ってしまわれましたから。　　　　　　　　　　　　　　（音楽）

11

Clint: (*siren*) Where are we headed? He didn't say which airport.

Guth: Just a hunch. The commercial airfields are all covered. But there's a little private field out here I remember. Hasn't been used in years.

Clint: That'll be the one.

Guth: They didn't have too much of a start on us. Maybe we'll make it in time. Step on it, Corporal.

Corp: Wide open, Major.

Guth: How'd he sound? Did he say who had him?

Clint: No, all he got out was airport and something about an ink...

Corp: Major, Mr. Clinton. There's a tail light up ahead. Must be another car, going like the devil.

(11)

クリントン： 　（サイレン音）どこへ向かってるんです？ 教授はどの空港かは言いませんでしたよ。

ガスロ： 　直感だよ。一般の飛行場はみな監視されてるが，ここには確かプライベートな飛行場があったはずだ。何年も使われていないがね。

クリントン： 　じゃ，きっとそれですね。

ガスロ： 　奴らが動いてからそんなに時間は経っていないはずだ。うまく行けば間に合うかもしれん。アクセルをふかすんだ，伍長。

伍長： 　もう全速力です，少佐。

ガスロ： 　教授はどんな様子だった？ 誰につかまったか君に話したか？

クリントン： 　いえ，ただ空港としか言いませんでした。それからインクがどうとか……。

伍長： 　少佐，クリントンさん，前にテールライトが見えます。別の車ですね，狂ったように飛ばしてる。

Guth: You're right. I see it. They're turning into the airfield. C'mon, faster.

Corp: Hold everything. Look up ahead. They're switching the floodlights on at the field. There's the plane down at the other end, all warmed up and ready to go. We'll never make it on the road. Hang on, I'm going through the fence. (*loud noise*)

Guth: What's the matter? Get going.

Corp: Sorry, sir. I must have cracked the axle. (*sound of airplane*)

Guth: They're taking off. Get out the submachine gun.

Clint: You can't. Barnhouse is in that plane. You'll kill him.

Guth: We've got to take that chance. That plane's headed straight for us. Hit the dirt! Get that gun working, Corporal. Aim for the propeller. (*sound of plane and machine gun*)

ガスロ： 　そうだな，見えるぞ。曲がって飛行場に入って行く。おい，もっとスピードを出せ！

伍長： 　ちょっと待って，前を見てください。飛行場の照明が点灯しますよ。向こうの端に飛行機がある。エンジンをかけて離陸しようとしてます。道路を走っていたんじゃ間に合わない。しっかりつかまってください。フェンスを破りますよ。（大きな音）

ガスロ： 　どうしたんだ，前進しろ！

伍長： 　すみません，車軸が折れたようです。（飛行機の音）

ガスロ： 　離陸してしまうぞ。マシンガンを出せ。

クリントン： 　だめです。教授も乗ってるんですよ。巻き添えになってしまう。

ガスロ： 　危険は承知の上だ。飛行機はまっすぐこちらに向かってる。伏せろ！　マシンガンの準備はまだか，伍長！　プロペラを狙え。（飛行機とマシンガンの音）

Corp: Couldn't get 'em, Major.

Guth: Well, there goes the old boy.

Corp: I'll get through to Air Patrol, sir. Maybe they can intercept the plane.

Guth: Not a chance. By the time the pilot got off the ground, the plane would be out of range. No, we've lost Barnhouse, and nothing can save us now. (*noise of psychic static*) Hey, what... (*explosion*) What hit me? Clinton, are you all right?

Clint: Yeah, sure. The, the plane. It's gone.

Guth: I know. Barnhouse blew it right out of the sky. He wouldn't let himself be taken alive.

Clint: Boy. He really did it the hard way. Poor guy. He shouldn't have had to be a hero. All he ever wanted was peace.

Guth: Peace! What's that? Now the arms race will start all over again. With Barnhouse gone, what's left to stop it?

(*music*)

伍長：　　　だめでした，少佐。
ガスロ：　　残念，取り逃がしたか。
伍長：　　　航空パトロールに連絡します。迎撃してくれるかもしれません。
ガスロ：　　無理だな。パイロットが離陸する頃にはもう射程外だろう。残念だがバーンハウスはもう戻らない。もうおしまいだ。（念動波の音）おや，あの音は……（爆発音）何があったんだ？　クリントン，君は大丈夫か？

クリントン：　ええ，大丈夫です。ひ，飛行機が吹っ飛んだんです。
ガスロ：　　そうか。バーンハウスが撃墜したんだ。生け捕りにはされまいとね。

クリントン：　残念だ。本当につらい道を選んだんですね。かわいそうに，なぜ教授が自分の身を危険にさらさなくちゃならなかったんだ，ただ平和を求めていただけなのに。
ガスロ：　　平和？　冗談じゃない。これで軍拡競争は一からやり直しだ。バーンハウスがいなくなった以上，これを止められる者はもういないんだ。　　　　　　　　　　　　　　　　　　（音楽）

12

Clint: So, they brought me back here to the professor's old study to dictate this report. I'm sitting here at his desk and it's just the way he left it — papers all over. Even his old pair of dice. (*rolls dice*) Arthur Barnhouse is dead. That's going to be good news for some people when they find out. The sabre rattlers of the world will be busy, as of tomorrow morning, getting ready to whoop up another war. I'm afraid they're in for a little surprise.

(*clock chimes three times*) It's 3 a.m. now, and before morning comes, I intend to vanish, disappear completely. That's the last that anybody will ever see or hear of me — directly. That's why I want to tell you, now. I've been looking at the new inkwell here on the desk. The professor's last words were something about an inkwell. And in it I found a little scrap of paper. Just a few words, but they complete the note I showed the major. The note that didn't make any sense. The whole thing makes sense now. Professor Barnhouse may be dead. But you

(12)

クリントン： 　こうして彼らは私を教授のかつての研究室に連れ戻し，私はこの報告書を口述している。私は今，教授のデスクに向かって座っている。すべては教授が残したままだ。書類は散らかり，教授のサイコロ2つもそのままだ。（サイコロを振る音）アーサー・バーンハウスは死んだ。人によってはこのニュースを歓迎する者もいるだろう。世界中のタカ派の連中は，明日の朝から次の戦争に備えて忙しく立ち回ることだろう。しかし，彼らのあてはきっと外れるに違いない。

　（時計のチャイムが3度鳴る）午前3時だ。夜が明ける前に，私は姿をくらますつもりだ。人が直接私の姿を見たり，声を聞いたりすることは2度とないだろう。だからこうしてあなた方に話しておきたいのだ。私はじっとデスク上の新しいインク瓶を眺めている。教授は最後にインク瓶について何か言おうとしていた。そして，インク瓶の中には小さな紙切れがあった。書かれていたのはほんの数語だったが，これは少佐に見せたメモを補うものだった。意味をなさなかったあのメモ。完成したメッセージは，今やはっきりとした意味を持っている。バーンハウス教授は亡くなったが，まだバーンハウス効果が消滅したわけではないのだ。あなた方に話しかけている間中，私は実験を続けてきた。そしてついに，あ

haven't heard the last of the Barnhouse Effect. Not yet. I've been experimenting while I've been talking to you. And now the time has come for me to say goodbye. (*rolls dice*) You see, I've just rolled my fiftieth consecutive seven.   (*music*)

THE END

なた方に別れを告げる時が来た。(サイコロを振る音)実はちょうど今,50回続けて7を出したところなのだ。(音楽)

終

＜イングリッシュトレジャリー・シリーズ㉑＞
バーンハウス教授の決意

2006年10月20日　初版発行Ⓒ　　　　（定価はカバーに表示）

訳　者　吉村順邦
発行人　井村　敦
発行所　㈱語学春秋社
　　　　東京都千代田区三崎町2-9-10
　　　　電話（03）3263-2894
　　　　FAX（03）3234-0668
　　　　http://www.gogakushunjusha.co.jp
　　　　こちらのホームページで，小社の出版物ほかのご案内をいたしております。
印刷所　文唱堂印刷

落丁・乱丁本はお取替えいたします。